W9-AYO-638

Beans

Heinemann Library
Des Plaines, Illinois

Roz Denny

© 1998 Reed Educational & Professional Publishing
Published by Heinemann Library,
an imprint of Reed Educational & Professional Publishing,
1350 East Touhy Avenue, Suite 240 West
Des Plaines, IL 60018

Designed by Celia Floyd
Illustrations by Barry Atkinson, pp. 12, 21, 24, 26, 28; Oxford Illustrators, p. 15
Printed in Hong Kong / China

02 01 00 99 98
10 9 8 7 6 5 4 3 2 1

Library of Congress Cataloging-in-Publication Data

Denny, Roz.
    Beans / Roz Denny.
      p.   cm. — (Food in focus)
    Includes bibliographical references and index.
    Summary: Describes how these edible seeds are grown all over the
world and the healthy, popular dishes made from them. Includes
recipes and experiments.
    ISBN 1-57572-653-X (lib. bdg.)
    1. Cookery (Beans)—Juvenile literature.   2. Beans—Juvenile
literature. [1. Beans.] I. Title. II. Series.
TX803.B4D45 1998
641.6'565—dc21   97-44108
                                          CIP
                                          AC

Acknowledgments
The Publishers would like to thank the following for permission to reproduce
photographs:
Birds Eye Wall's, p. 13; Anthony Blake, p. 9 top right (Graham Kirk), p. 9 top left
(Andrew Sydenham); Gareth Bowden, pp. 9 bottom, 10, 11, 14, 16, 17, 18, 19, 20, 22,
23, 25, 27, 29; e.t. archive, p. 5; Trip, p. 4 (R. Dury), p.7 (TH Foto-Werbung).

Cover photograph: Trevor Clifford

Every effort has been made to contact copyright holders of any material reproduced
in this book. Any omissions will be rectified in subsequent printings if notice is given
to the Publisher.

> Some words are shown in bold, **like this**. You can find
> out what they mean by looking in the Glossary.

Contents

* * * * * * * * * * * * * * * * * * * *

Introduction   4

History of Beans   6

Beans Around the World   8

Types of Beans and Other Legumes   10

Growing Beans and Other Legumes   12

Baked Beans   14

How to Cook Beans   16

The Soybean   18

Beans and Health   20

An Experiment—Bean Sprouts   22

Recipe: Quick Chilli con Carne   24

Recipe: Tuna and Two-Bean Salad   26

Recipe: Pea, Tofu, and Avocado Dip   28

Glossary   *30*

More Books to Read   *31*

Index   *32*

Introduction

New varieties of peas grow along the ground in fields

Scientists use the term "leguminous" to classify vegetables that are flowering plants which produce their own edible seeds, e.g., peas, lentils, beans. These vegetables grow all over the world, and almost every country has popular dishes using them.

Legumes can be eaten young and fresh (sometimes even before the seeds have formed inside the pods) or grown until they are larger and can be dried and stored.

All the countries in the world have beans and other legumes in their **cuisines**. They can be grown in large fields or small kitchen plots. They are simple to pick by hand and will dry on the plant if necessary, ready to be packed away in sacks.

Beans and other legumes are also one of the healthiest foods people can eat. There are no known religious taboos against eating them. Their value has been recognized since ancient times. In old civilizations, the dead were even buried with dried beans so they had good food to take with them into the next world.

Stories about beans

Throughout history, everyone could eat beans because they were easy to grow and store, so it is perhaps not surprising there are so many legends and sayings about beans. Here are just a few.

- When you are down on your luck, with no money, you could say you "haven't a bean."
- Beans were so common that if a person said he "couldn't give two beans" about something it meant he didn't care.
- Identical twins are often described as looking like "two peas in a pod."
- Heavy, damp fogs are often called "pea soupers" as they are very thick.
- Bean feasts were held in honor of the ancient Greek god of beans. Nowadays some countries call parties with lots of food "bean feasts."
- In England, sometimes friends call each other "old bean" as a friendly greeting.

A bean fairy tale

Bean plants were known to be good at growing tall and strong without much tending. Young Jack in the fairy tale found his magic bean just grew and grew. Its thick stalk grew into a giant's kingdom in the sky. Jack used it to climb up into the giant's castle, and then stole his gold harp. He scampered back down the bean stalk, chopped it down, and gave his poor mother riches beyond her dreams. All the happened by growing one bean!

There are many stories about the growing power of beans.

History of Beans

The Ancient World

Beans and other legumes originated in different parts of the world and spread as people began to travel and live in new lands. The oldest legume is thought to be the lentil. This was first cultivated around 7,000 B.C. in the ancient world of Mesopotamia, in Syria, and in the Near East from where it traveled to ancient Rome. *Lens* is the Latin word for lentil. The glass in eyeglasses is known as a lens because it is the same shape. Other legumes that first sprouted in the Middle East were peas, chickpeas, and broad beans.

Many Middle Eastern and Indian dishes still use chickpeas (such as in *hummus*), broad beans, and lentils in much the same way as they did thousands of years ago. The Ancient Egyptians were fond of a type of broad bean called *fava*, which is still eaten in large amounts in the Middle East. The Greeks and Romans would offer *fava* beans at funerals as food for the dead person to take into the next life.

Did you know?

Beans and legumes were so highly regarded in Ancient Rome that prominent political families had pea or bean surnames—Fabius (from faba/fava), Lentulus (lentil), Piso (peas), and Cicero (chickpea).

Bean dishes are still eaten by Egyptians today.

6

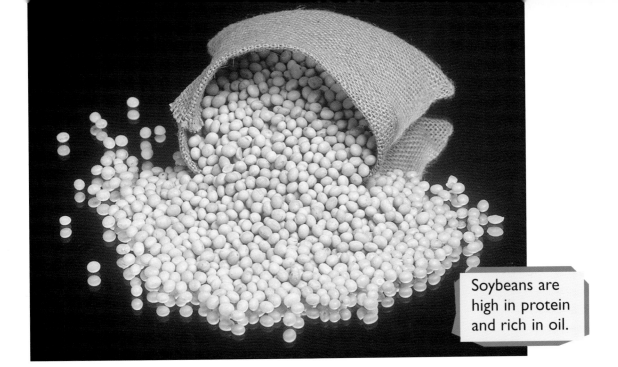

Soybeans are high in protein and rich in oil.

Beans in the Orient

The "king" of legumes, the soybean (sometimes called soya bean), originated farther east, in China and Japan. Many uses were developed for this highly nutritious food. Soybeans have the highest amount of protein of all beans and are also rich in oil and vegetable fat. This bean is a relative newcomer in the legume world as it was first used in about 1,000 B.C. Today it is grown in many countries, especially the United States, where it was introduced in the nineteenth century by a famous sailor, Commodore Perry. Mung beans also come from China and Japan. One of the main ways of serving mung beans nowadays is as bean sprouts (see page 22).

In the New World

In Central America the native beans were lima beans (butter beans) and small white oval beans later called navy beans because they were popular with sailors. When they were brought over to Europe, cooks called them "haricot" beans because they were cooked in a pot with a cut of lamb called haricot. The haricot, or navy bean, is one of the beans used to make baked beans.

Did you know?

Peas were used by the Czech monk Gregor Mendel in the mid-nineteenth century to demonstrate his theories on the science of genetics (how all living things inherit looks, color, shape, etc.)

Beans Around the World

There is a great variety of beans and other legumes grown around the world, and almost as many different ways of cooking and serving them.

In the Americas

Lima beans, navy beans, kidney beans, and chickpeas are among the most popular and are grown in several different sizes and colors. The Mexicans, for example, love to use red and black kidney beans in a dish called *chilli con carne* with meat and spices (see page 24). They also like to fry cooked red beans until they are softened to a puree, which they call *frijoles refritos*.

In North America, Native Americans taught the first settlers how to cook many dishes using beans to help them through the long, hard winters. One of these is a delicious bean soup called *succotash*, made of lima beans and sweet corn, which is still cooked and eaten today.

India—the land of dhals

Cooks in India call legumes *dhal*. Examples are *masoor dhal*, *toor dhal* and *urd dhal*. They are cooked to a spicy puree, often with added vegetables, and eaten with delicious flat breads called *nans* or *chapatis*. Many people on the Indian subcontinent are **vegetarians** and *dhals* are an important part of their healthy diet. Legumes are also used to make flours. One of these, called gram flour, is made into thin, crisp pancakes called poppadums.

From country kitchens to top restaurants

European cooks have been very clever using beans and legumes over the centuries. Yellow peas were wrapped in a bag and cooked with boiling hams to be served as pease porridge. In Spain, chickpeas are cooked in spicy casseroles and even *paellas*. France has a tasty slow-cooked dish of beans, salt pork, and spicy sausage called *cassoulet*. Top restaurant chefs all over the world like to cook with puy lentils grown in the volcanic soil of the Massif Central region of France. These small blue-green lentils are said to look like tiny volcanic rocks.

Cassoulet is very tasty eaten with chunks of crusty baguette.

Another favorite Caribbean dish is "Hoppin John" made with black-eyed peas.

Caribbean color

If you go on holiday to the West Indies you will most probably be served a dish called simply "rice 'n' peas." All the islands seem to have their own favorite versions. Most use gunga peas but on some islands they like to use red kidney beans and flavor the dish with coconut and a herb called thyme.

Beans in the East

China and Japan have used soybeans for thousands of years and make many other products with them. One of these is a **curd** called tofu, which looks like a soft cheese and is very high in protein and low in fat. Soybeans are also mashed up and left to **ferment** to make soy sauce or fermented beans. There are even recipes for sweet cakes using beans.

Soybeans are crushed and made into tofu.

Types of Beans and Other Legumes

Peas and beans are known as legumes because the seeds grow in pods. Sometimes legumes that are part of the bean family are called "peas." The names can be very confusing! In the end it doesn't matter as most of them are cooked and eaten in similar ways.

> ### Did you know?
>
> *The word legume comes from the French verb* legere, *"to pick," because such plants are picked by hand.*

Peas

The different types of pea include:

- garden peas—perhaps one of the most popular frozen vegetables, sold in packages
- split peas, green and yellow—used to make thick winter soups
- chickpeas—also known as *garbanzos* in Spain and parts of Central America

To shell fresh peas, choose only young, fresh pods that are newly picked, ideally ones grown in a garden. Put a bowl on your lap, take up a pea pod and press down on the tip of the pod opposite the stalk. The pod should pop open. Then you can push the fresh peas out into the bowl. Fresh peas are delicious eaten raw—try a few!

Peas are pushed from the pods after they have been popped open.

Beans

Phaseolus is the general botanical name for beans. It means "boat-shaped," which is similar to the shape of a bean pod. The most common bean was first grown about 7,000 years ago in southern Mexico. Many other popular beans have been developed from this one strain. One of the most well–known in the Americas is the lima bean, named after Lima, the capital of Peru. The lima bean was taken to Africa by slave traders on their return journey from the New World. The bean has become a popular legume there. Other varieties of beans from the New World are kidney beans, pinto beans, black beans, and black-eyed peas (really a bean!).

Fresh legumes (peas and beans) are ready for picking in the early to mid-summer. Apart from peas and baby peas, known as *petit pois*, we can buy peas still in their pods, to be eaten whole, such as snow peas and sugar snap peas, which do indeed snap when bent in half.

Fresh beans are not usually podded. Instead they are picked young and tender and are topped and tailed—that is, the stalk and tip are pinched off. Small bean pods are cooked whole, larger ones are sliced before cooking. There are many varieties of fresh green beans. In France, the most popular are called *haricots vert*. In the United States, string beans are great favorites especially with home gardeners. String beans are served whole or sliced diagonally ("french cut").

String beans can be eaten whole with their pods.

Growing Beans and Other Legumes

Although peas and beans are grown worldwide in thousands of varieties, they are slightly difficult plants to grow because they are easily attacked by pests and diseases. Seeds of legumes are sown in the early spring and like rich, well-drained soil. Once sprouted, the seedlings need regular watering and a certain amount of warmth. Some varieties do not tolerate frosts and can only be grown in parts of the world that are frost-free during spring. When the pods have become swollen with peas, inside they are ready for harvesting. This is often in the mid to late summer.

Legumes grown for sale as dried beans or peas are picked and dried in the country of origin, then shipped to whatever country wishes to buy and repack them for sale.

The inside of a bean

All legumes are made up of two halves, called cotyledons. These store protein and energy for the new seedling when it sprouts. They are held together by a seed coat, and between them nestles the embryo, which includes the root, stem, and first pair of leaves for the new plant. Where the seed joins the pod is the hilum which looks a bit like a belly button.

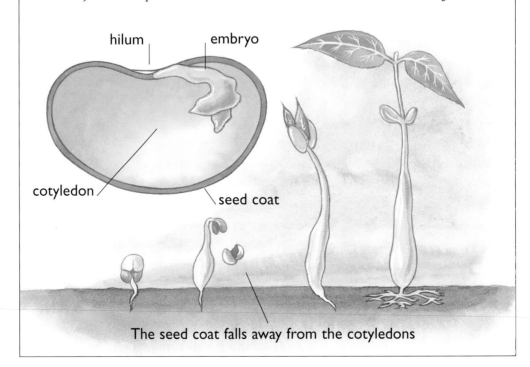

hilum embryo

cotyledon seed coat

The seed coat falls away from the cotyledons

Big companies use huge machines called "viners" to harvest peas.

Legumes in home gardens

In gardens and smaller farms legumes are planted to grow around sticks, or supports, and are picked by hand. As soon as the pods start to develop after flowering, each flower's growing tips are pinched off. This allow the growing plant to put more energy into forming the pods. Some leguminous plants are quite attractive and gardeners like to grow them over arched frames.

The pea harvest

Peas and beans grown commercially need to be harvested quickly by machines. As a result, certain varieties have been developed to grow along the ground without supports. Peas grown for freezing, for example, are at their best flavor and texture for only a few hours and must be harvested almost instantly. Company technologists check on the tenderness of ripe peas using a machine called a tenderometer.

When farmers decide the time is right for harvesting, huge combine harvesters called pea viners roll out into the fields, whatever the time of day or night. These pea viners can pick the plants and pod the peas at the same time. The peas are rushed to the factories to be **blanched** and frozen. That is why frozen peas often taste better than fresh peas. They can literally be picked and frozen within $1\frac{1}{2}$ hours.

Baked Beans

The Puritan settlers in Massachusetts were very devout and would not allow anyone to work on Sundays. People were supposed to spend their time praying or resting. That also meant no cooking was allowed. So on Saturday nights the women would take large pots of soaked beans, together with salt pork, mustard, "black strap" molasses and spices, to the baker's shop to cook in the bread ovens. As many Puritans lived in and around Boston, this dish became known as "Boston baked beans."

The first canned Boston beans were made in 1875 by a company called Burnham and Morrill who gave them to the crews on their fishing boats. In 1895, Mr. H. J. Heinz of Pittsburgh, Pennsylvania developed and sold the first cans of "Oven Baked Beans with Pork and Tomato Sauce." Six years later the first cans were imported into Great Britain and sold as gourmet food. Eventually they became more popular and cheaper. During World War II the pork was left out of the recipe because of rationing. Nowadays hundreds of millions of cans of baked beans are sold each year.

Baked beans are a very healthy food as they are high in protein and fiber and low in fat. It is also possible to buy low-sugar and low-salt baked beans or beans in a variety of other flavors.

Baked beans are very good for you.

14

How baked beans are made

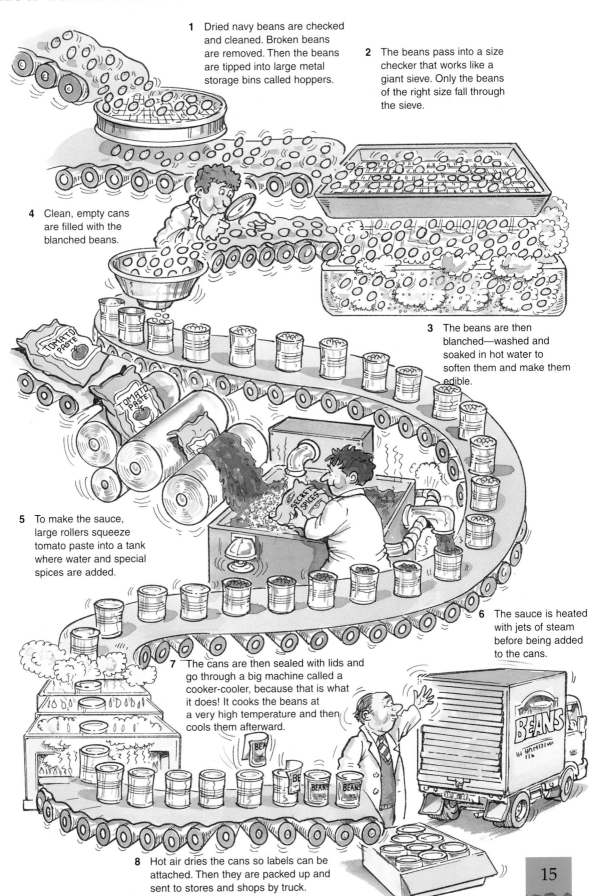

1. Dried navy beans are checked and cleaned. Broken beans are removed. Then the beans are tipped into large metal storage bins called hoppers.

2. The beans pass into a size checker that works like a giant sieve. Only the beans of the right size fall through the sieve.

3. The beans are then blanched—washed and soaked in hot water to soften them and make them edible.

4. Clean, empty cans are filled with the blanched beans.

5. To make the sauce, large rollers squeeze tomato paste into a tank where water and special spices are added.

6. The sauce is heated with jets of steam before being added to the cans.

7. The cans are then sealed with lids and go through a big machine called a cooker-cooler, because that is what it does! It cooks the beans at a very high temperature and then cools them afterward.

8. Hot air dries the cans so labels can be attached. Then they are packed up and sent to stores and shops by truck.

How to Cook Beans

Fresh peas and beans are easy to cook. They just need a little preparation, "topping and tailing" (cutting the top and bottom off.) They should be cooked in a little boiling water for a few minutes, then drained, and perhaps tossed with a little butter or olive oil.

Dried beans and other legumes have had their water removed by drying, so they need to have water added to soften and plump them up again. This can best be done by soaking them first, which helps shorten the cooking time.

Dried beans also need to be boiled hard for a good five to ten minutes depending on the variety. This is important for kidney beans, because they contain a substance that is mildly poisonous and can give you a stomach ache. This can be destroyed by boiling the beans for ten minutes. They can then be simmered gently until softened.

How to soak dried beans

Allow about 1½ ounces (¼ cup, 40 g) per person.

Place the beans in a large bowl and cover with cold water that is at least 2 inches (5 cm) deep above the beans. Stir once and leave for about eight hours or overnight. It is probably a good idea to cook at least 9 ounces (1½ cups, 250 g) of dried beans at a time then store any leftovers in the refrigerator or freezer.

If you are in a hurry you can cover the beans with boiling water and then leave them to cool for one hour.

Soaking dried beans helps to shorten the cooking time.

Tip

Chefs do not add salt to beans while they are cooking as it is supposed to toughen the skins. Some food scientists do not agree. Maybe you would like to experiment. Try cooking some beans with a little salt and some without.

Kidney beans are best boiled hard for ten minutes and then simmered until tender.

Cooking dried beans

Cooking times vary according to the bean or legume, from 20 minutes right through to 1½ hours.

Check the instructions on your package or in a cookbook first.

1 Drain the soaked beans in a colander and place in a large saucepan. Cover again with cold water about 2 inches (5 cm) deep above the beans. Do not add any salt, although you might like to add a sliced carrot, an onion, and two large bay leaves.

2 Bring slowly to a boil. Boil hard for ten minutes and then turn the heat down and cover with a lid. Simmer the beans—or lentils or peas—for the time required. You may find a little scum forms on the top. This is normal. It is simply extra proteins seeping out of the beans. Scoop it off with a slotted spoon if you don't like the look of it.

3 Test the beans by picking out one or two with a fork and biting into them. When they are soft, drain carefully in a colander and toss with some salt and pepper plus butter or olive oil. They are also delicious with some fresh chopped parsley.

17

The Soybean

Historians think it is no coincidence that the spread of soybeans in Asia happened at about the same time as the spread of the religion of Buddhism, which encouraged a **vegetarian** diet.

The Chinese learned centuries ago that soybeans have a great many uses—apart from being eaten as beans.

- The quality of the protein in soybeans is almost as good as that of meat which makes them a good meat substitute.
- They can be crushed to make good healthy cooking oil and margarine, and they are also useful for making soaps and paints.
- Soybeans make excellent food for cattle.
- The beans can be **fermented** and salted to flavor and preserve them. On their own, simply cooked, they do not have much flavor.
- They can be mashed and made into milk and cream for people who cannot or do not want to drink cows' milk.
- Soy milk can be made into a high protein **curd** called tofu, which has many uses in the kitchen.
- They can be made into soy sauce.

Today around three–quarters of the world's crop of soybeans is grown in the U.S. although most of it is for commercial use, not for food.

Soybeans are very versatile.

Tofu can be fried in hot oil so it becomes crispy on the outside.

Soybean curd

This food may have been invented in China around 200 A.D. Bean curd, also known as tofu, is quite bland on its own but it takes on other flavors easily and can be pressed to give it the texture of cheese. This means it can then be **marinated** in other flavors, or smoked like bacon.

To make bean curd, the beans are soaked, mashed, and then cooked in high-pressure steam. The mashed beans are **filtered** to give milk, then a chemical called calcium sulfate is added to the milk to turn it into curds. These can be drained and pressed into cakes and then turned into bean curd, or tofu.

The Chinese and Japanese like to fry cubes of pressed tofu. It becomes quite crisp on the outside and is delicious served with a stir-fry of vegetables. Tofu that is not pressed but still quite creamy is called silken tofu. This can be used in soups, drinks, or as an alternative to creamy milk.

Soy sauce

Soy sauce can be made in two ways. The quick way is carried out in a factory. The longer method involves **fermenting** the soybeans over several months. This type of soy sauce is known as "naturally brewed" and has a slightly stronger flavor and slightly sweeter taste.

To make naturally brewed sauce, the beans are crushed and roasted, then mixed with roasted wheat. They are left to ferment, when they bubble slightly and develop flavor. In this process, a harmless mold develops, rather like rind on a cheese, which is harmless as well.

The mixture is then mixed with **brine** and natural yeasts and left again to ferment for six months to a year. After that it is filtered and **pasteurized** (that is, heated) to help it store well.

Beans and Health

Dried beans and legumes can be called nature's little storehouses. They are very nutritious, inexpensive, and easy to grow. They store well and can be cooked simply in a pot over an open fire or on a hot plate.

What's in a bean?

Pulses contain three important nutrients—proteins, carbohydrates, and **fiber**.

We need proteins for our bodies to grow strong. Proteins are made up of **amino acids**. Meat and fish are complete proteins because they have the right number of amino acids, but many peoples of the world are not able to—or do not want to—eat meat and fish. They need to eat different vegetable protein foods to make complete proteins.

These dishes all have complementary proteins.

Although legumes are good sources of vegetable proteins, they are still not complete proteins. Grains and starchy foods, such as rice and cornmeal or pasta, potatoes, and bread have the proteins missing from legumes. When these two groups are eaten together in the same meal they make up the complete protein requirement.

Without realizing why, people throughout the centuries have eaten dishes with legumes and grains (food made from cereal plants)—for example, chilli beans and rice, cannellini beans and pasta, *dhals* and rice, pea soup with crusty bread, tofu and rice, and *hummus* and pita bread. These dishes are very healthy. Can you think of more?

Our bodies only need a moderate amount of protein foods to grow, depending on our age and size. If we eat more than we need, the rest is used up as energy or stored as fat. A medium portion of beans— about 2 to 3 tablespoons—with a larger portion of grains or a nice chunk of crusty bread—is enough for a well-balanced meal.

Beans are also a good source of carbohydrate, which we need to give us energy. The skins give us a lot of fiber to help keep our intestines healthy.

Food pyramid

Scientists tell us we must think of our daily diet as being like a pyramid. At the bottom are starchy foods and we should get about half our **calories** from these foods. Fruit and fresh vegetables should form the next largest part of our diet, followed by protein foods such as beans and legumes, meat, fish, and dairy products. At the very top we can have a small amount of sugar and fat.

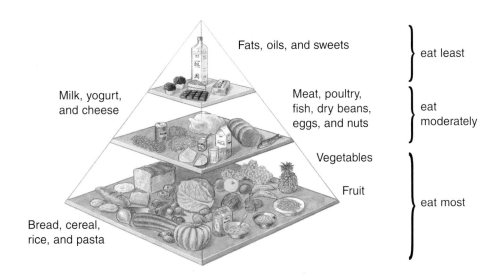

An Experiment—Bean Sprouts

How to sprout beans

When dried beans are soaked and drained but left damp, they will start to sprout, or "germinate," and new little plants will grow.

You can germinate bean sprouts easily.

It is easy to make your own bean sprouts at home. If you have a proper sprouter, which is a series of slotted plastic trays that fit on top of each other, then you can sprout three types of seeds at once. Otherwise, use a jam jar for one type of bean at a time.

You will need:

- a large, clean, glass jam jar
- water
- a clean piece of cheesecloth (or a new, clean dish towel)
- a thick elastic band
- beans or other legumes of your choice

Choose from green lentils, chickpeas, soybeans, aduki beans, black-eyed peas, lima beans, and mung beans.

Use dried beans or legumes that are well within their "sell-by" date. Those that do not start to sprout after three days are too old and should be thrown away.

What to do:

1. Put 2 to 3 tablespoons of beans in a clean jam jar and cover with **tepid** water to a depth of 2 inches (5 cm) Cover the top with a small sheet of cheesecloth or thin dish towel and secure with an elastic band.
2. Leave overnight to soak and swell, then tip the water out through the cloth. Fill with more water, filling through the cloth, almost to the top and tip the water out again. *This is important—it washes the beans clean of any gases.*
3. Lay the jam jar on its side in a light warm place but not in direct sunlight, i.e., not on a sunny windowsill. Shake the beans down to form an even layer.
4. Rinse again two to three times a day, through the same cloth top. Do not take it off.
5. After two days or so, you should start to see the beans crack open and sprout. New life—very exciting! Some beans may sprout more quickly than others, so be patient.
6. The sprouts are ready to eat when they are three times the length of the bean. Rinse and drain one more time then remove the cloth top.

If you can't eat all the sprouts at once, cover and store them in the refrigerator to stop their growing. Eat within two days, either fresh in a salad or lightly cooked, for example in a stir-fry.

How to serve bean sprouts

You can add your own bean sprouts to almost anything. They are wonderful in salads, or try them in omelettes, sprinkled on top of spaghetti instead of cheese, mixed with mayonnaise as a sandwich filling or stirred into casseroles just before serving. Soon you will come up with lots of your own ideas. Sprouted chickpeas, for example, can be eaten just like popcorn or peanuts as healthy nibbles.

- If you eat the newly-sprouted bean before the first leaves open, you will have a lovely crunchy fresh vegetable that is full of healthy nutrients. Health food stores sell a good range of ready-sprouted beans. The most popular are mung beans.
- It's good fun to have three or four jars of different beans all sprouting at once.

Bean sprouts are full of fresh vitamins.

Recipe: Quick Chilli con Carne

Originally from Mexico, the name of this dish means "chilli with meat." The recipe also includes red kidney beans, cooked in a spicy tomato sauce. When served as a **vegetarian** dish with cheese instead of meat, it is called *chilli con queso* (*queso* is the Spanish word for cheese.) Either way, you can serve it with plain boiled white rice although pasta and mashed potatoes are also good. Ask an adult for help before you start cooking.

Chilli con carne
Serves 4 people

You will need:
Ingredients

- 1 tablespoon vegetable oil
- 17.5 oz (500 g) lean ground beef or turkey
- 1 onion, chopped
- 1 fat clove of garlic, crushed
- 1 tablespoon ground paprika
- 2 teaspoons (10 ml) mild chilli powder
- 1 teaspoon (5 ml) ground cumin
- 1 teaspoon (5 ml) oregano
- 2 tablespoons (30 ml) tomato puree
- 2 cups (450 ml) stock
- 15 oz (420 g) of red kidney beans
- salt and ground black pepper

Equipment

- large frying pan with lid
- large stirring spoon or spatula
- cutting board
- sharp knife
- measuring spoons
- garlic press
- measuring cup
- can opener

What to do:

1. Heat the oil in a large frying pan and then fry the ground beef or turkey, stirring it often with a spoon to break up any lumps.
2. When the meat is brown and crumbly, stir in the onion and garlic and cook for another 5 minutes.
3. Mix in the spices—paprika, chilli, cumin, and oregano. Cook for another 2 minutes.
4. Stir in the tomato paste, stock, and kidney bean liquid from the can.
5. Season lightly, bring to the boil, then cover and turn the heat down to a simmer. Cook for 20 minutes then stir in the kidney beans. Return to the heat and simmer, uncovered, for 5 more minutes. Serve in bowls.

Chilli con carne

Recipe: Tuna and Two-Bean Salad

• •

In France and Italy, beans are often used in salads as in this recipe from the countryside around the Mediterranean Sea. This recipe uses fresh beans as well as dried beans mixed with tuna fish. It is very colorful and tasty. You can serve it as a light meal with French Bread. Ask an adult for help before you start cooking.

Tuna and two-bean salad

Serves 4 people

You will need:

Ingredients

- 4 ½ oz (¾ cup, 125 g) navy beans, soaked
- water
- 4 ½ oz (¾ cup, 125 g) whole green beans
- 6 oz. (200 g) can tuna fish in oil
- 1 celery stock
- 2 medium-sized onions
- 2 medium-sized tomatoes
- small handful fresh parsley sprigs
- sea salt and ground black pepper

Dressing

- 2 tablespoons (30 ml) olive or sunflower oil
- ½ teaspoon garlic salt
- 1 teaspoon (5 ml) French mustard
- ½ teaspoon sugar
- 2 tablespoons (30 ml) wine vinegar

Equipment

- large saucepan with lid
- cutting board
- sharp knife
- colander
- big mixing bowl
- can opener
- mug
- kitchen scissors
- table fork
- jam jar
- serving dish

What to do:

1 Soak the navy beans in water overnight or for at least four hours. Drain the soaked beans. Put them into the saucepan and cover with cold water at least 2 inches (5 cm) above the beans. Bring to a boil and boil for 10 minutes. Then turn the heat down and simmer until the beans are soft, about 50 minutes.

2 Meanwhile, cut the ends off of the green beans and cut them into 1-inch (2.5 cm) lengths. Add to the simmering navy beans for the last 5 minutes of cooking, then drain both. Put the beans into a bowl and add a pinch of both salt and pepper.

3 Open the can of tuna fish carefully and drain the oil into the beans, stirring well. Leave the beans to cool.

4 Flake the tuna fish with a fork and set aside in the refrigerator. Cut the celery into thin slices and the onions into small chunks. Cut the tomato into quarters then cut out the stalk end. Cut each quarter into half so you have eighths of tomato.

5 Now carefully mix the tuna, celery, onions, and tomato together in a big bowl. Keep chilled until the beans are quite cool then stir them in as well.

6 Put the parsley sprigs into a mug and using kitchen scissors, snip them into smaller sprigs. They do not have to be too fine. Toss them into the salad.

7 Put the dressing ingredients into the jar. Shake well, then stir into the tuna and beans. Serve chilled in a large attractive dish.

Tuna and two bean salad

Recipe: Pea, Tofu, and Avocado dip

• •

This is a modern international dish, mixing foods from the East and West. The tofu represents the East, the peas and avocados are from the West, and traditional Worcestershire sauce comes from England. Serve with Mexican style corn tortilla chips. You will need a food processor for this recipe so ask an adult to help you.

Pea, tofu, and avocado dip

Serves 4 to 6 people

You will need:

Ingredients

- 8 - 10 oz. (250 g) frozen peas, thawed
- 3 ½ oz. (100 g) tofu , firm or silken
- juice of 1 lime or ½ a small lemon
- sea salt and ground black pepper
- 2 salad onions
- 1 clove garlic
- ½ teaspoon (2 ml) ground cumin
- 1 teaspoon (5 ml) Worcestershire sauce
- 1 ripe avocado

For the garnish

- a few peas
- 1 small tomato, sliced
- parsley, chopped

Equipment

- lemon juice squeezer
- food processor
- cutting board
- sharp knife
- teaspoon
- plastic scraper
- pretty bowl for serving

What to do:

1 Put the peas, tofu, lime or lemon juice, and seasoning into a food processor.
2 Peel the salad onions and chop them roughly. Peel the garlic clove, chop it roughly, and put it into the processor along with the onions, cumin, and Worcestershire sauce.
3 Cut through the avocado lengthways until you can feel the pit, then twist both halves and pull them apart. Take out the pit with a teaspoon and scoop the flesh into the processor.
4 Now switch on the processor and puree until smooth, turning off once or twice and scraping the mixture down the sides. Spoon into a pretty bowl and garnish with some peas, sliced tomatoes, and a sprig of parsley.

Pea, tofu, and avocado dip

Glossary

amino acids   vital acids that make up a protein

blanch   to dip prepared vegetables for a minute or two in boiling water to cook them partially so they can be prepared for freezing. After blanching, the vegetables are quickly dipped in ice cold water to cool them

brine   a mixture of salt and water; sometimes other flavorings are added as well

calories   a measure of energy in food. Foods such as lettuce have few calories, while high-fat foods such as butter will have more calories for the same weight

cuisine   type of cooking that is specific to a country

curds   an ingredient that has formed into small soft lumps and can be pressed into a solid. In cheese-making, milk is turned into curds when a substance called rennet is stirred into it. To make tofu, soy milk can be turned into curds as well.

ferment   to undergo a chemical change in which carbon dioxide gas and alcohol are produced as byproducts

fiber   material found in the cell walls of all plants, including vegetables, legumes, fruits, cereals, nuts, and seeds. Our bodies do not break down and digest dietary fiber but it makes our waste products soft so that they pass through our digestive system easily. Nowadays dietary fiber is known as non-starch polysaccharide

filter   to drain a liquid through a fine sieve to make it clear

marinate   to soak a food in a sauce of well-flavored liquids and oils. The soaking liquid is called a marinade and may consist of soy sauce or oils, vinegars, lemon juice, herbs, and spices

pasteurize   to reduce the amount of bacteria in liquids, like milk, by heating

tepid   a temperature that is neither hot nor cold. If a liquid is tepid it feels lukewarm

vegetarian   a person who chooses not to eat meat or fish. Some religions require that their followers do not eat meat or fish

More Books to Read

Jennings, Terry. *Beans.* Ada, OK : Garrett Educational Corporation, 1995.

Johnson. *Potatoes, Tomatoes, Corn, & Beans.* New York: Simon & Schuster Children's Books, 1997.

Miller, Susanna. *Beans & Peas.* Minneapolis, MN: Lerner Publishing Group. 1990.

Index

Amino acids   20
Ancient world   4, 5, 6

Baked beans   7, 14-15
Beans   4, 5, 7, 11, 12, 13, 16, 26
Bean sprouts   6, 22, 23
Butter beans   7, 22

Calories   21
Carbohydrates   20, 21
Cassoulet   8
Central America   7
Chickpeas   6, 8, 10, 22
Chilli con carne   8, 24
China   7, 9, 19
Commodore Perry   7
Cooker-cooler machine   15
Cooking times   17
Cotyledons   12

Dhal   8, 21

England   5
Europe   7-8
Experiment 22-23

Fava beans   6
Fiber   20
Food pyramid   21
France   8, 11, 26
Frijoles refritos   8

Germinating beans   22
Grains and legumes   21
Gunga peas   9

Haricot beans   7, 11, 26
Healthy eating   21
Hilum   12

India   6, 8
Italy   26

Japan   7, 9, 19

Kidney beans   8, 11, 16, 24

Legumes   4, 6, 10, 12, 13
Lentils   6–8, 22
Lima beans   7, 8, 11, 22

Mange touts   11
Mendel, Gregor   7
Mesopotamia   6
Middle East   6
Mung beans   7, 22
Mushy peas   11

Navy beans   7
Near East   6
North America   8
Nutrients   20

Paella   8
Pea soupers   5
Peas   4, 6, 10, 11, 12, 13, 16, 28
Peru   11
Petit pois   11
Proteins   7, 12, 14, 20, 21
Pulses   7, 8, 22

Recipes,
    Pea, Tofu, and Avocado   28
    Quick Chilli con Carne   24
    Tuna and Two-Bean Salad   26
Religion   4

Snow Peas   11
Soy sauce   18, 19
Soybean curd   9, 18, 19, 21, 28
Soybeans   7, 9, 18, 22
Spain   8
Succotash   8
Syria   6

Tenderometer   13
Tofu   9, 18, 19, 21, 28

United States   11, 14

West Indies   9

Yellow peas   8